FRUIT OF THE SPIRT

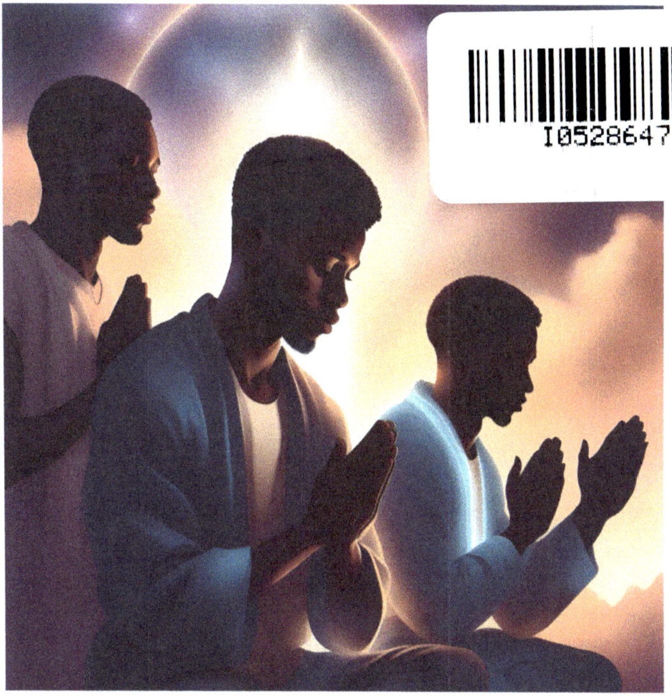

MEDITATION BOOKLET

By Karajah Yashar

WWW.BSPBOOKS.COM

FRUIT OF THE SPIRIT: MEDITATION BOOKLET

ISBN: 978-1-962691-42-0

FIRST EDITION: OCTOBER 2024

Table of Contents

The Fruit of Love

"HE THAT LOVETH NOT KNOWETH NOT GOD; FOR GOD IS LOVE."
1 JOHN 4:8

"BELOVED, LET US
LOVE ONE ANOTHER:
FOR LOVE IS OF GOD;
AND EVERY ONE THAT
LOVETH IS BORN OF
GOD, AND KNOWETH
GOD."
1 JOHN 4:7

4

"HUSBANDS, LOVE YOUR WIVES, EVEN AS CHRIST ALSO LOVED THE CHURCH, AND GAVE HIMSELF FOR IT"
EPHESIANS 5:25

5

IF YE LOVE ME, KEEP MY COMMANDMENTS. JOHN 14;15

6

The Fruit of Joy

"REJOICE IN THE LORD ALWAY: AND AGAIN I SAY, REJOICE."
PHILIPPIANS 4:4

7

"HITHERTO HAVE YE ASKED NOTHING IN MY NAME: ASK, AND YE SHALL RECEIVE, THAT YOUR JOY MAY BE FULL."
JOHN 16:34

8

"NOW THE GOD OF
HOPE FILL YOU WITH
ALL JOY AND PEACE IN
BELIEVING, THAT YE
MAY ABOUND IN HOPE,
THROUGH THE POWER
OF THE HOLY GHOST."
ROMANS 15:13

"WHOM HAVING NOT
SEEN, YE LOVE; IN
WHOM, THOUGH NOW YE
SEE HIM NOT, YET
BELIEVING, YE REJOICE
WITH JOY UNSPEAKABLE
AND FULL OF GLORY"
1 PETER 1:8

10

The Fruit of Peace

"NOW THE LORD OF PEACE HIMSELF GIVE YOU PEACE ALWAYS BY ALL MEANS. THE LORD BE WITH YOU ALL."
2 THESSALONIANS 3:16

"THOU WILT KEEP
HIM IN PERFECT
PEACE, WHOSE MIND
IS STAYED ON THEE;
BECAUSE HE
TRUSTETH IN THEE."
ISAIAH 26:3

"FOR GOD IS NOT THE AUTHOR OF CONFUSION, BUT OF PEACE, AS IN ALL CHURCHES OF THE SAINTS."
1 CORINTHIANS 14:33

13

"BLESSED ARE THE
PEACEMAKERS: FOR
THEY SHALL BE
CALLED THE
CHILDREN OF GOD."
MATTHEW 5:9

14

The Fruit of Long Suffering

"AND WE KNOW THAT ALL THINGS WORK TOGETHER FOR GOOD TO THEM THAT LOVE GOD, TO THEM WHO ARE THE CALLED ACCORDING TO HIS PURPOSE."
ROMANS 8:28

15

"THE LORD IS NOT SLACK
CONCERNING HIS
PROMISE, AS SOME MEN
COUNT SLACKNESS; BUT IS
LONGSUFFERING TO US-
WARD, NOT WILLING THAT
ANY SHOULD PERISH, BUT
THAT ALL SHOULD COME
TO REPENTANCE."
2 PETER 3:9

"AND NOT ONLY SO, BUT
WE GLORY IN
TRIBULATIONS ALSO:
KNOWING THAT
TRIBULATION WORKETH
PATIENCE; AND PATIENCE,
EXPERIENCE; AND
EXPERIENCE, HOPE"
ROMANS 5:3-4

17

"SUBMIT YOURSELVES
THEREFORE TO GOD.
RESIST THE DEVIL,
AND HE WILL FLEE
FROM YOU."
JAMES 4:7

18

The Fruit of Gentleness

"THOU HAST ALSO GIVEN ME THE SHIELD OF THY SALVATION: AND THY GENTLENESS HATH MADE ME GREAT."
2 SAMUEL 22:36

19

"A SOFT ANSWER
TURNETH AWAY WRATH:
BUT GRIEVOUS WORDS
STIR UP ANGER."
PROVERBS 15:1

20

"AND THE SERVANT OF THE LORD MUST NOT STRIVE; BUT BE GENTLE UNTO ALL MEN, APT TO TEACH, PATIENT"
2 TIMOTHY 2:24

"HE SHALL FEED HIS FLOCK
LIKE A SHEPHERD; HE
SHALL GATHER THE LAMBS
WITH HIS ARM, AND CARRY
THEM IN HIS BOSOM, AND
SHALL GENTLY LEAD THOSE
THAT ARE WITH YOUNG."
ISAIAH 40:11

22

The Fruit of Goodness

"SURELY GOODNESS AND MERCY SHALL FOLLOW ME ALL THE DAYS OF MY LIFE; AND I WILL DWELL IN THE HOUSE OF THE LORD FOR EVER."
PSALMS 23:6

"HE HATH SHEWED THEE, O
MAN, WHAT IS GOOD; AND
WHAT DOTH THE LORD
REQUIRE OF THEE, BUT TO
DO JUSTLY, AND TO LOVE
MERCY, AND TO WALK
HUMBLY WITH THY GOD?"
MICAH 6:8

"A GOOD MAN OUT OF THE
GOOD TREASURE OF THE
HEART BRINGETH FORTH
GOOD THINGS; AND AN
EVIL MAN OUT OF THE
EVIL TREASURE BRINGETH
FORTH EVIL THINGS."
MATTHEW 12:35

25

"LET LOVE BE WITHOUT
DISSIMULATION.
ABHOR THAT WHICH IS
EVIL; CLEAVE TO THAT
WHICH IS GOOD."
ROMANS 12:9

The Fruit of Faith

"NOW FAITH IS THE SUBSTANCE OF THINGS HOPED FOR, THE EVIDENCE OF THINGS NOT SEEN."
HEBREWS 11:1

"THAT YOUR FAITH
SHOULD NOT STAND
IN THE WISDOM OF
MEN, BUT IN THE
POWER OF GOD."
1 CORINTHIANS 2:5

"AND JESUS ANSWERING SAITH
UNTO THEM, HAVE FAITH IN
GOD.FOR VERILY I SAY UNTO YOU,
THAT WHOSOEVER SHALL SAY
UNTO THIS MOUNTAIN, BE THOU
REMOVED ...AND SHALL NOT
DOUBT IN HIS HEART, BUT SHALL
BELIEVE THAT THOSE THINGS
WHICH HE SAITH SHALL COME TO
PASS; HE SHALL HAVE
WHATSOEVER HE SAITH."
MARK 11:22-23

"BUT WITHOUT FAITH IT
IS IMPOSSIBLE TO
PLEASE HIM: FOR HE
THAT COMETH TO GOD
MUST BELIEVE THAT HE
IS, AND THAT HE IS A
REWARDER OF THEM THAT
DILIGENTLY SEEK HIM."
HEBREWS 11:6

The Fruit of Meekness

"BLESSED ARE THE MEEK: FOR THEY SHALL INHERIT THE EARTH."
MATTHEW 5:5

31

"TO SPEAK EVIL OF NO MAN, TO BE NO BRAWLERS, BUT GENTLE, SHEWING ALL MEEKNESS UNTO ALL MEN."
TITUS 3:2

"NOW THE MAN MOSES
WAS VERY MEEK, ABOVE
ALL THE MEN WHICH
WERE UPON THE FACE
OF THE EARTH."
NUMBERS 12:3

33

"BUT LET IT BE THE HIDDEN MAN OF THE HEART, IN THAT WHICH IS NOT CORRUPTIBLE, EVEN THE ORNAMENT OF A MEEK AND QUIET SPIRIT, WHICH IS IN THE SIGHT OF GOD OF GREAT PRICE."
1 PETER 3:4

34

The Fruit of Temperance

"TEACHING US THAT, DENYING UNGODLINESS AND WORLDLY LUSTS, WE SHOULD LIVE SOBERLY, RIGHTEOUSLY, AND GODLY, IN THIS PRESENT WORLD"
TITUS 2:12

"BE SOBER, BE VIGILANT;
BECAUSE YOUR ADVERSARY
THE DEVIL, AS A ROARING
LION, WALKETH ABOUT,
SEEKING WHOM HE MAY
DEVOUR:
1 PETER 5:8

36

"BUT PUT YE ON THE
LORD JESUS CHRIST,
AND MAKE NOT
PROVISION FOR THE
FLESH, TO FULFIL THE
LUSTS THEREOF."
ROMANS 13:14

37

"...giving all diligence, add
to your faith virtue; and to
virtue knowledge;
And to knowledge
temperance; and to
temperance patience; and
to patience godliness"
2 Peter 1:5-6